HOW TO MANAGE YOUR MONEY

Top Guide: Stop Impulsive Spending, Pay off Debt Fast and a Live a Rich Life

"The Path to Your Financial Freedom Starts Here"

By May Collins

Contents

Introduction

Welcome to How to Manage Your Money, where your path to financial freedom begins.

Do you want to learn proven techniques that will help you manage your money the smart way?

Do you want to be able to relax with the assurance that all your needs today and in the future can be sorted with ease?

You are in the right place

We have all gone through tough financial times. Moments where credit card debt and borrowing money seem like the only way to keep our financial life afloat. Such situations leave us feeling ashamed and worried about our financial future.

Maybe, you have tried using a budget but it still does not seem to work.

This book will equip you with tools, knowledge and solutions that work.

You will learn the seven money lessons that are easy to implement. I promise you that if you read every page of this book, and follow the advice here, you will be headed to a world where you will never be a slave to your money.

CHAPTER 1

The Budgeting Lesson

"A budget tells us what we can't afford, but it doesn't keep us from buying it."

William Feather

WHAT IS A BUDGET?

How much money do you make? How do you spend it? How much is allocated to repay debts? How much do you save?

Budgeting helps answer these questions.

A budget is a way of keeping track of how much money comes in and how you spend it. Budgeting is, therefore, a process that entails a plan on how all the money that you make will be spent. Having a spending plan helps you determine early enough if the money will be enough to meet all the needs you have. In the case where that money be enough, then you will need to prioritize your spending by focusing on the things that are more important. Ultimately, a budget not only helps you make smarter financial choices but also gives you a sense of control over where your money goes every month.

Some budgets work, but others fail. A budget that works requires hard work, tweaking, plenty of practice and a lot of trial and error. If yours is giving you a hard time, don't ditch it, implement new tools and techniques until you find the right balance.

The best way to develop a spending plan is to have a written monthly budget that you can easily evaluate as time elapses.

Later in this chapter, I will show you how to develop a spending plan that REALLY works. So, keep reading.

WAYS THAT BUDGETING CAN BUY YOU HAPPINESS

Interestingly, most people associate budgeting with plenty of restrictions, lots of hustle and headaches. But that is not the case. Using a proper budget, will buy you happiness. In fact, it will grant you a better life. Below are five benefits of budgeting that will help you look at a budget in a new light.

Benefit #1: Budgeting eliminates overspending

You will agree with me that failure to budget makes you overspend. Yes, because spending can be too easy. Online shopping makes it even easier to spend. Just a few clicks and an array of merchandise is delivered to your doorstep. The result is an empty bank account, a huge credit bill and the grief of being in too much debt.

The good thing with budgeting is that it does not prevent you from enjoying the things you want in life (After all, You only Live Once), rather, it helps you to keep track of your spending habit.

Benefit #2: Budgeting shows your financial position

Unless you have a budget, you can never be sure of your spending compared to your income. Besides helping you understand where you stand financially, budgeting further enables you to know whether you are living within your means or on borrowed money. It also shows you where your income comes from, where it goes and whether you are spending it wisely.

Benefit #3: Budgeting helps you set, commit and track the progress of your goals

The moment you prepare a workable budget, it shows you how much you need for expenses and what to set aside as savings to buy a car, house, vacation or as emergency funds. It, therefore, allows you to commit to these financial goals thus preventing you from spending on things that do not contribute to attaining your goals. Now, you will have a choice to buy random items for instant gratification or wait to feel a lot better when you finally achieve your financial goal. Remember to make the budget a live document that you can refer to now and then. Do not put it in a drawer because you might end up losing it and start forgetting your financial goals. This budget is your guide to financial freedom, and you, therefore, need to keep checking your progress. When you constantly check it out, this is enough incentive to keep you moving forward and attaining your financial objective.

Benefit #4: Budgeting makes you the pilot of your money

Mac Duke once said that: *"if you don't take care of your money, then the money won't take care of you."*

Think about this; at the start of the week, you had $500 in the bank account. But five days later, you don't understand where it went or what happened to it. All you are sure about is that your account now reads $0.

Does the above sound familiar? Probably, Yes!

But this would not have happened if you had a well laid budget.

Budgeting instills discipline. Budgeting controls how you spend every single cent. Budgeting also helps you manage your money instead of the money controlling you.

When you have a well laid out budget, it will save you the stress of gradually adjusting your lifestyle because of lack of funds. It also helps you decide on whether to sacrifice short term spending like buying a burger daily at the expense of a long-term benefit such as buying a home.

Benefit #5: Budgeting helps you save more

It is no-brainer that people who have no budget tend to save little or nothing at all. When you budget, it means you are assigning your money to do other important things. Money is therefore automatically put into an emergency account or any other specified account. This will ultimately help you plan for your expenses in advance thus preventing you from dipping into your savings kitty.

Benefit #6: Budgeting helps you minimize debts

The moment you clearly understand how much money comes in and how much goes out, it becomes easy to plan your expenses. You will always pay bills on time, and that means living a debt free lifestyle.

Debts are however not a bad thing. They just need to be necessary and affordable at the time. Budgeting will show you how much debt you can afford. A debt that will not stress you or paralyze your lifestyle.

Benefit #7: Budgeting will lower your stress

Imagine it is getting close to Thanksgiving Day. You have a pretty big family, and they all expect some sort of gift from you. There is also a gift exchange at your work place and several other parties you are expected to attend. Before you know it, a whopping $2000 is gone. This is an extra $1000 more than your monthly expenses.

A few days later, your car breaks down, and the mechanic needs $500. You get to your bank account, and the balance reads $300. So, your only option is to get a loan from a friend or get into credit card debt.

That can be stressful. Right?

But this would not have happened if you had been using a budget. It would have been easier to allocate money for the gifts and the parties. Even the car could have been easily budgeted for as an emergency or miscellaneous case.

The situation would have been better if you had budgeted for things like savings for Thanksgiving, Christmas and other holidays. The money for the gifts would have been there already without requiring you to dig deep into your pockets.

So, save yourself some stress by prioritizing budgeting in your financial life.

THE REASONS YOUR PREVIOUS BUDGETS FAILED YOU

Methodical money tracking can be tedious. Recording every cup of coffee and packets of milk purchased can easily find you resenting the activity. Sometimes you will get home, and the last thing you want to handle are spreadsheets and numbers. Gradually, it is easy to find yourself cheating on your budgeting by labeling figures incorrectly. Eventually, you will give up on budgeting, and that might 'just' be the beginning of your financial goals' death.

Personally, budgeting is a lifestyle. I am addicted to spreadsheets, and I am a serial number cruncher. I love how I can set my own financial goals and commit to achieving them. However, this does not come without a share of its own challenges. Although I love how a budget organizes my money, I hate adjusting my lifestyle and spending to meet what the spreadsheet dictates.

I am sure that you can relate to my experience. It is also likely that you have given budgeting a chance in the past, but it failed you terribly. Budgeting is supposed to work. If it failed, you did not do it the right way.

As a serial budget maker, I have discovered seven reasons that make a budget fail and tips on how to fix them. So, find out where you have been going wrong in your budget.

Reason #1:   Being too restrictive

When you are desperate to save money, you can easily be tempted to strip down your spending to the bare minimum. If you are lucky, it can work out, and you get to enjoy a hefty surplus at the end of your saving period. However, to most people, it doesn't work. Executing a very restrictive budget is stressful as you try to challenge yourself to live within a limit you definitely cannot. In fact, most of us do not even reach halfway without tossing the entire budget in the garbage. Because it did not work.

TIP; be realistic and adjust your budget accordingly. Slash a few areas at a time without attempting to give your lifestyle a complete overhaul at the same time. Well, a huge surplus at the end of your saving period looks good on paper, but if you cannot hack it in practice, then it is all a futile exercise. For instance, your intention might be to save $3000 by the end of the month. If it sounds too restrictive, then spread the saving period over two months.

Reason #2:   Failure to set realistic goals

A goal keeps you motivated to stick to your budget. However, while getting rich at the end of your saving period is an admirable goal, make sure that goal is realistic and achievable. For instance, you cannot set a savings goal of $5000, yet you are still paying off debts on top of other regular expenses.

TIP; set achievable goals. If your target is to save or pay off a huge chunk of debt, plan to divide the specific amounts in the given period. You can also set other mini goals along the way (if your situation allows), to help you stay strong. Remember to reward yourself (just modestly) when you finally reach the finish line.

Reason #3: Your family is not onboard

Your family can either make or break your budget. You might be determined, disciplined and geared towards reaching a financial goal. But all that depends on whether or not you are getting support from your family. Your spouse, children and any other family members you live with must be on board if your budget is to become a success.

TIP; It's time to have the big money talk in the family. Sit everyone down, discuss your financial goals together. Be well prepared with all the numbers handy. Help them understand that a budget will not necessarily alter your lifestyles, but it will act as a roadmap for the family financial position. You will be amazed at how positively they will embrace your proposal.

Reason #4: You do not plan for emergencies

Emergencies do not happen all the time, and you can, therefore, be tempted not to allocate funds for them. Whether or not you have had emergency cases for the last two months, the simple rule is that a budget is incomplete without an emergency allocation. It can be so hurting to see your carefully detailed budget derailed by an accident that breaks your dog's jaw, the need to have your toddler's tonsils removed or a new transmission for your car. Before you know it all the money is gone before you have paid the monthly bills.

TIP; always build an emergency fund that contains total savings of at least six months living expenses. If you are yet to build the emergency fund, devote your budget into establishing it by setting a target. Consider an emergency fund as an insurance policy. The premiums are still yours even if you will never file a claim.

Reason #5: You get impatient

I am the one person who gets impatient on almost everything in life. Sometimes, I get impatient of my own budget. I obsessively get excited to see how much I have saved and if I am a millionaire yet. Maybe, you do the same too. But the truth is, budgeting requires patience, time and trial, and error until you produce significant results.

TIP; be patient and give your budget enough time. The first few months should be a beta test for your budget. These months can be tough, and if you are not careful, you can easily give up. Try making simple adjustments every month when things do not go smoothly. Ironing out creases and seeing real changes in your budget can take time. So, go easy, be yourself and be PATIENT.

Reason #6:   You are lazy

Yes, you are lazy indeed. I am also lazy at times. Recording every single coin that enters your pocket and then recording all those coins as they are spent is tedious. Right?

Budgeting requires devotion. Because budgeting is all guesswork until you fully put it into practice. The moment you draw up a budget, you submit yourself into a life of numbers. You must enter all the utility bills, credit card statements and every other expense (no matter how petty), if you want to develop an accurate spreadsheet. If you have not touched your budget since you first drew it weeks ago, then that is why it is probably not working out well.

TIP; revisit your budget weekly. Devote a few minutes to adjust a few items like fluctuating utility bills, extra furniture, new commissions and anything else you did not plan for at the beginning of the month.

Reason #7:   Maybe you just HATE budgets

Budgeting is not for everyone. Budgets are a lifestyle choice, they are personal, and they are driven from within. Some people find it a huge hurdle tracking their spending effectively. It's understandable if you fall into this category.

However, before concluding that budgeting is just not your thing, you might need to explore other techniques of managing your money. Yes, because spreadsheets and columns can suck big time.

TIP; seek alternative budgeting methods that resonate with your lifestyle and income. For instance, if keeping a budget doesn't seem to work for you, try withdrawing just enough money for your expenditure. You can withdraw money for a week, two weeks or even a month. This kind of regimen is only workable if you are disciplined. Otherwise, you might withdraw enough money for a week just to spend it within a day. If this method still doesn't sound good to you, test a few budget alternatives and settle for one that works for you.

COMMON MYTHS ABOUT BUDGETING

There are plenty of untrue misconceptions about budgeting. People who are 'anti-budgeters spread these myths,' and their primary aim is to distract focused people from reaching their financial goals. Do not allow these misconceptions stop you. Do not let them to prevent you from doing the best thing that will secure your financial future. After reading and understanding what these myths are, you will always be too smart to fall for them.

Myth #1:   A budget will deny me the things I want

A good budget is not restrictive. In fact, a reasonable budget will make it possible to buy things you have always wanted over a long term.

It's tempting to shelf budgeting for another month, or another year or even forgetting it entirely. It's also possible to say that, 'I'll buy what I want now and worry about the future later.

Myth #2:   I make a lot of money, so there is no need for a budget

Budgets are not for poor people. Neither are they for people who live paycheck to paycheck. Budgets are for everyone. Even if you have enough money to cover all your expenses, plenty of savings and no debts whatsoever, you should never stop maintaining a budget.

Let me give you a short relatable story.

I once had a friend, let's call her Mary. She was a successful woman making over $100,000 a year. She lived in a high-end neighborhood, drove an expensive car and went on vacation to all-inclusive resorts in Miami. Well, by the look of it, she was doing awesome. But let's open the curtains and look at her life more closely.

Mary's net pay was about $80,000 after income taxes. She spent $10,000 of this money on vacation every year. That left her with about $70,000 left over which translated to $5,833 per month.

Her mortgage balance was $300,000, and even with the lowest interest rate of 3.44%, she coughed at least $1,333 monthly payments. And remember it would take her 30 years to pay off the mortgage entirely. She now had $4,500 per month remaining.

Property taxes for that beautiful house stood at about $4,000 per year, an average of $333 per month

This simply means that she only had $4,167 per month remaining.

She still owed money for that nice car she drove. So, let's add monthly payments of $771.

Mary had two children who attended sporting activities at a high level. The cost of lessons, uniform, and other equipment set her back another $1,200 every month.

After these deductions, she had $2,196 remaining every month.

Lest we forget, Mary was still making payments for a students' loan from college which amounted to $500 a month.

So, in totality, she only had $1,697 left every month to feed her family, cover utility bills, cater for household expenses, build an emergency fund and save for her retirement.

By the time she paid all these things, was already dipping into credit and accumulating debt.

Whoops. Indeed, life doesn't look so good after all.

So, what can we deduce from this? Having a lot of money doesn't mean you should skip budgeting.

Mary is careless with her money. She goes on fancy vacations when she literally cannot afford it. She has no savings and slowly by slowly, she is getting herself into bad debts.

No matter how much money you have, things can easily get out of control. A budget will help you plan the money you have accordingly thus preventing you from extravagance and falling into bad debts.

Myth #3:   I earn too little, so I don't need a budget

Just as described above, a budget is for everyone. Whether you make too little or your bank account is overflowing.

It's tempting to skip budgeting when you earn just enough to keep you alive. But you will be shocked to realize that your earnings are not actually that little. Your money disorganization and overspending could have rendered it appear so.

But come to think of it, a well-designed and maintained budget makes you focused. It keeps you on track and motivates you to seek side hustles to keep your budget on track.

For instance, let's say you aim to save for a dream vacation, build an emergency fund or to buy a car. Maintaining a budget will ensure that every month, you set aside enough money to reach your goal. This way, you will avoid accidental spending on discretionary things.

Myth #4:   Budgeting is time-consuming

Not true. The initial drawing of a budget can take time, but after that, everything become more easy. You might even need at most 15 minutes a day to keep it going. If most of your expenses are on a weekly basis, then you might only need to check your budget once a week. So, it is a misconception that budgeting takes a lot of time.

WAYS TO HAVE MORE MONEY WITHOUT GETTING A PAY RAISE

It sounds impossible, but the easiest way to have more money is to avoid spending money that you do not have. You do not need a pay hike to be rich. All you need is to avoid making banks and credit companies rich. As we shall see, if you commit yourself to put what you have into good use, you will never be a victim of bad debts and unnecessary loans.

What are bad debts?

Any debt that does not make you more money except the interest accrued every month is bad debt. When you take a loan to purchase things that lose value quickly, depreciate fast and do not generate income in the long term, then that is bad debts too.

If you want to avoid bad debts, then go by this rule. If you cannot afford it and it's not a necessity, then do not buy it.

For instance, what is the essence of buying a TV screen at $3,000 on your credit card? And the screen will eventually cost you $4,000 inclusive of interest. Yet, the screen will never pay that balance on your card. And don't forget that, in a couple of years, the TV will have depreciated in value and will probably be out of style. That is an excellent example of a bad debt that can be avoided.

Avoid advertisements and salespeople who make us think that getting a loan to buy things we actually need is normal. No, it's not normal.

Credit companies and banks are only concerned with making money from the interest you will eventually pay in the long run. The truth is that bad debt can suck the life out of you. They are relentless. And they kill your ability to save.

So, which are the common sources of Bad debts (and how can you avoid them)

Source #1: Car Loans

Yes, you can afford the monthly payments, but imagine how much extra money you will be paying for that car. If you add all the interest payments, they add up to a huge amount.

If possible, pay off that loan as soon as you can. The interest you are paying is better used on other useful things in your life.

Figure this out. You decide to buy a nice car worth $40,000. You also manage to get a low interest of only 5% payable within five years.

Sounds very affordable, right?

But wait.

By the end of five years, you will have rendered to the bank a total of $5,290 as interest.

Say it with me, an extra $5,290 to an already established and affluent company.

This is money that could go towards other important expenses. The money could have eased your burden on food, clothing, and shelter.

Please note that I am not discouraging you from owning a car. Precisely a nice car. I am trying to make you see the sense of the huge interest that awaits you.

So, which options do you have?

- ✓ Do not buy a fancy car until you can afford it.
- ✓ Look out for a used car that you can afford (of course without taking a loan)
- ✓ Take out a savings plan and purchase that dream car as soon as you reach the savings target
- ✓ Consider, seriously, if you need a car. If you live in a place with a good transit system and can manage without one, then do not bother buying one.

A car comes with its share of costs that easily eat up a lot of money. From maintenance, repairs, gas to insurance, add the figures to determine if owning a car is worth it for you.

Source #2:   Furniture Loans

From time to time, we feel the need for a make over of our homes. Sometimes we can afford it. Other times, we may have to get a loan to buy new stuff or we simply ignore the need for a make over until a later date, when we can afford it.

I will tell you one thing; never get the temptation to take out a costly loan to purchase furniture. The salespeople will use all sorts of enticing language to have you bring home the newest furniture designs. They will even tell you to take the furniture home and pay off the costs within a year at no extra charge. And then you figure out it's a great deal since you will have an entire year to save up the money while enjoying the furniture at home.

But the reality is...

Every time you are home resting on that debt-ridden couch, you will have this fear hanging over your head.

What if you are unable to raise that money within a year? What if something unexpected happens and consumes up all your money? What if you are slapped with an outrageous rate of interest?

In truth, you would enjoy your furniture more if you paid in full. You would be assured that the couch is 100% yours with no strings attached.

So, what options do you have?

- ✓ Ask family and friends if they are getting rid of their furniture. You might get less used furniture at an affordable price that will not strain your bank account
- ✓ Check out garage sales and thrift stores for gently used furniture at awesome prices
- ✓ Embark on a savings plan to buy new furniture. You can purchase your furniture of choice once you meet your target

It's possible to live with less furniture and still be happy. If you read our book on decluttering you will understand this. Society gives us unnecessary pressure and expectations that we cannot afford. Some of these expectations are designed to encourage you to part with your money and make companies that make furniture richer. So, do not buy into this trick; unless you can honestly afford it.

Source #3:   Vacation Loans

Vacations are beautiful. It's a great time to bond with our families and take a break from our busy schedules. But taking a loan to take a vacation is not advisable. Do not allow credit companies and banks to convince you otherwise.

Vacation loans are worse than furniture loans. With the former, interest will start accruing from the day the money is deposited in your account.

During the vacation, you won't get to enjoy the finest bits with debt hanging over your head. It's even worse to imagine the amount of interest you will pay on your loan.

So, what options do you have?

✓ Save enough money to take a vacation.

✓ Never take a vacation until you can afford it

Source #4: Credit Card Debt

Credit makes our life easy. They are convenient when we need to pay up for things. However, when used carelessly they can cause stress to our lives. You need to pay off the accrued debts in full every month; otherwise, you will end up with outrageous amounts of interest that can be a real pain in your life.

The best way to avoid credit card debt is to determine how much you will pay in interest if you decide to take that route. The truth is that, if you do your calculations well, you will be shocked by the huge amounts you will end up wasting in the name of 'interests.' Credit card companies are money making businesses, which are looking forward to ripping your hard-earned cash.

Have a look at this simple example.

Let's say you want to purchase an item worth $3,000 that you would fund via a credit card debt. Assuming you will get a low interest payable in 22.1 years. That means you will be making monthly payments of about $60.

Sounds affordable, right?

But wait...

How much interest will you pay in the long run? At the end of 22.1 years, you'll pay a total of $7,000 in interest. Come to think of it, your initial $3,000 triples to over $10,000.

The thing is, by the time you are done paying the debt, the odds are the item you had purchased is already in rags.

So, what options do you have?

✓ If possible, avoid buying items on credit card debt

✓ If you must buy, then let it be something that gives you value for money and is worth the time you will be paying off the loan

✓ Use a credit card payment calculator for a reality check that will help you resist the temptation of accruing credit card debt

✓ Try saving up enough money for the item you need instead of purchasing it on credit card debt

HOW TO MAKE A BUDGET

There is a popular quote that states that the secret to getting ahead is getting started. Indeed, it's time for you to learn how to make an accurate, achievable and realistic budget.

I hope that you have keenly read the topics before this one. If you have, you already understand the essence of keeping a budget and how it can help you reach your financial goals. I also want to believe that you are armed with the knowledge of why some budgets fail, common misconceptions about budgeting and some of the ways you can implement to have more money even if your earnings are very little.

So, now you will learn how to make a super budget. A budget destined to work. But it's only possible if you are dedicated to making it a success.

The Tools You Will Need to Get Started

Interestingly, you do not need any fancy software and tools to take control of your money. In fact, the basic items you need are a notebook, pen, and calculator.

However, if you are not the kind of person who enjoys doing calculations by hand, then a computer will be necessary.

The internet is also home to hundreds of free money trackers that you can download and keep updating when need be. However, if you are skeptical about these third-party apps, you can still track your budget in the regular spreadsheets on Ms.Office or Open Office.

One last thing, this exercise might be tedious, but do not let this scare you off.

If you want a life that puts you in control over your hard-earned money, then this exercise is a necessary evil.

So, get comfortable, grab a bowl of popcorn and get ready for this great course. Remember to take a break when your mind gets exhausted. Stretch your limbs, take a walk, then come back and continue. Slowly but gradually, you will be through. And I promise you that the process will get easier once you have laid the foundation the right way.

Step-By-Step Guide To Creating Your First Budget

Preparing a budget can be very overwhelming. Maybe, this is the reason why only 40% of American families maintain workable monthly budgets. However, despite all the energy required, the exercise is all worth it.

When I created my first budget a couple of years ago, I knew the exact amount I was making, but I was not sure how much I was spending. I had never thought of breaking the expenses down to determine where my money was going.

It was after I formulated the first budget that I realized I was spending on things I could not really afford. If this is the first time you are making a budget, this step-by-step guide will definitely make the process less tedious.

Step #1: Determine how much you have

Start by checking your savings and all accounts to determine the money that they hold. This should include the interest rates and expenses each of them has. Be sure to note this down since we shall use it to determine your net worth later.

Step #2: Determine how much you make

When on a salaried pay scale, it is easy to determine your monthly income. For the self-employed or those who work on an hourly basis, it can be a little difficult since income rises and falls unpredictably.

The best way to find how much you make monthly is by determining an average income that you receive. You can take figures of the last 6 to 12 months to get an average.

Step #3: Determine your debts

Here, you will need to determine your monthly recurring debt payments. This includes car loans, mortgages, child support, student loans, credit card debt and any other debts that you pay monthly. Get the total debt of all the above to determine how much you are required to pay every month.

Step #4: Determine your recurring monthly expenses

Monthly expenses are hardly regular in most households. Therefore, the best way to determine this figure is by getting an average.

Ensure that you keep receipts, utility bills and every other expense that arises during the month. For easier sorting, divide the expenses into two categories; Fixed and variable. The fixed expenses are those that remain the same each month. They include rent, car payments, internet charges, trash collection fee, credit card payments among others.

Variable expenses on the other hand change from one month to the other. They include items such as groceries, entertainment, car fuel, gifts, eating out and other discretionary items.

Be sure to determine an average amount for each of these categories.

Step #5: Determine your expenses over income

Start by totaling your monthly income and then the monthly expenses (debts included). If your result shows more income than expenses, kudos! You are off to a good start. It means you can now take the extra amount to your retirement scheme or other savings plan.

However, if the result shows more expenses than income, you will need to make adjustments to your life.

Step #6:   Determine your net worth

Your net worth equals how much money you owe (debts plus expenses) subtracted from how much money you have. Your net worth is an eye-opener. It allows you to understand your financial situation. The first time I created a budget, my net worth gave a negative figure. It was an indication that I was living far beyond my means and something had to change.

Step #7:   Enter this information into a database

As I mentioned earlier, there are many online budgeting tools and money trackers you can use to prepare your budget. Personally, Microsoft Excel works best for me because it allows a great deal of flexibility compared to other software programs.

However, be free to choose what works best for you. The main goal is to create wealth and to keep out of financial trouble.

After entering all the data into the spreadsheet, you will be able to figure out whether you have been overspending or under spending. It will also allow you to determine if you have been living a lie or within your means.

The next step will, therefore, require you to adjust your monthly expenses to live a less stressful life.

Step #8:   Making adjustments

The main goal in any budget is to have the income column equal to that of the expenses. Ideally, this means that all your income has been accounted for and budgeted for various expenses and saving goals.

If the spreadsheet proved that you are overspending, you will need to cut on your monthly expenses. Start by having a look at your variable expenses. Most of them are want-to-have expenses that can be easily avoided. For instance, you can skip a movie night in favor of a movie at home. You can also skip buying lunch in favor of carrying packed lunch to the office. Also, while the internet is a need at home, do you really need the fastest option available?

If the figures are still not adding up, you can try adjusting the variable expenses. For instance, you can downsize to a more affordable house to save on rent.

The key is to determine your needs vs. the wants. Bring your family aboard to determine the adjustments all of you can put up with to reach the financial goal. The decisions come with a big tradeoff, so be sure to weigh your options the right way.

These adjustments may appear insignificant, but the small savings eventually add up to a lot of money. So, do not overlook them.

Step #9:   Make your adjustments based on reality

Life is full of surprises. Food prices keep fluctuating, gas prices get hiked now and then. Today you are working, but tomorrow you are fired. You get a pay hike today and tomorrow you face a pay cut. So is life.

Always make your adjustments to your budget when setbacks creep in. You cannot continue living under the same lifestyle when money is no longer coming in. You must adjust to reality.

Step #10:   Track, monitor and be loyal to your budget

It's vital that you review your budget regularly to make sure that you are on the right track. Keeping it in check takes less than an hour every week. As time goes, you might only need at most 15 minutes to keep it up to date.

You can also compare your budget with that of people at a similar level with you. You might adopt a few elements that can be very beneficial to making your budgeting process a success.

After the first month of successful budgeting, sit down and determine your progress. Compare the actual expenses versus your budget. This will show you where you did well and what to improve. Remember to make any adjustments if need be.

CHAPTER 2

The Savings Lesson

Saving must become a priority, not just a thought. Pay yourself first.

Dave Ramsey

WHAT IS SAVING?

Saving simply means putting some money aside for future use. In better words, it is spending postponed. This is because the money you set aside as savings may relate to your end of year vacation, your children's education fees or maybe your retirement in 30-years.

The good thing with savings is that it can help you achieve your financial goal without getting bogged down into debt. Whether you want a new car or stereo, a down payment for a nice house or your dream car, you can get it through saving.

Unfortunately, life has become too expensive hindering our ability to save. Most of us spend beyond what we earn and it's therefore difficult to save as much as we would like. But that does not mean we cannot save.

This chapter is meant to teach you ways you can make saving possible despite how much your income is. However, saving is a broad topic, and much of it will be partially covered in the other chapters.

HOW TO SAVE FROM A PAY RAISE OR NON-PLANNED INCOME?

For many months (or years) you have been living on a meager salary. Then one day your boss wakes up on the right footing and doubles your salary.

Kudos! Landing a pay raise is a big achievement, and it makes you feel valuable in the company.

You might also get lucky and receive an unexpected income; like winning a jackpot, inheritance or tax refunds.

The temptation to live a little bit better will keep hanging on your head. You would love to move to a bigger house, buy a new car, treat your family to a vacation and treat yourself to everything you have always wished for.

But come to think of it, is this the life you would live if you were to get a pay raise more often. Of course not!

According to financial experts, you should save 50% of your salary increase. They also suggest that 90% of any non-planned income should be put into savings or investment.

Here are tips to make good use of those extra bucks

Tip #1:   Start building an emergency fund

As we earlier discussed, an emergency fund is a necessity, and every person or family needs one. This is the money you withdraw for medical emergency, car and home repairs or when you unexpectedly lose your job.

Although we shall discuss an emergency fund in the next topic, it is worth reminding you that an emergency fund needs to cover at least six months of your living expenses. Therefore, using your pay raise to build your family's emergency fund is a pretty good idea.

Tip #2:   Contribute to your retirement

Think about your ripe years. The best time to make those years golden is by saving for them today. Well, you might already have a retirement savings plan but increasing the premiums is not a bad idea. So, use part of your pay raise to grow your savings for the retirement plan.

Tip #3:   Pay yourself

Yes! Do something for yourself. You worked very hard to earn a pay raise. Set aside part of the raised income to treat yourself. You can buy that pair of shoes you have eyed for so long or some new furniture for your home. You can also go out on vacation (why not?). However, if you have some other itching priorities, the vacation can be scheduled for a later date. But that does not mean putting it off completely. If you can faithfully shelf a small portion every month, you will be able to go for that vacation after the savings accumulate.

Tip #4:   If possible maintain your spending

Lifestyle creep is the enemy of accumulating wealth. It's tempting to better your lifestyle when you start earning more. This can result in overspending on discretionary things. If possible, maintain your spending.

By shelving the desire to spend your extra bucks today, it means you will soak them into savings that will grow in value. In the long run, this will provide financial resources that you can use in the future to improve your living standards.

ESTABLISHING AN EMERGENCY FUND

We have discussed emergency funds several times in the previous topics. We have also highlighted the importance of an emergency fund and cases that should be catered for by this kitty.

But for the sake of this chapter, an emergency fund is money set aside to cover large unexpected expenses. This could be medical emergencies, appliance repairs, car fixes and in the most unfortunate cases, loss of a job.

An emergency fund will help you avoid borrowing and will keep you afloat during desperate times without relying on credit cards and high-interest loans.

But how much money is enough for an emergency fund?

We are all different, and our family needs also vary. Therefore, there is no standard amount we can say is enough for the emergency kitty. The best judgment is based on your living expenses. A stable emergency fund should be enough to cover three to six months of your living expenses. If you can save more, then the better.

Remember to put money for this kitty in an account that is easy to access because an emergency can strike at any time. The account should, however, be separate from the bank account you use daily to prevent you from dipping into your reserves.

How do you build an emergency fund?

- ✓ Start by setting a monthly goal. This will motivate you and get you into the habit of saving on a regular basis. You can authorize your bank to put up a standing order that transfers funds to your emergency kitty, every time you receive a paycheck
- ✓ Put up a piggy bank at home. Use it to keep loose change and when it fills up, move the money to the emergency kitty. If you do not carry cash, make use of a mobile savings app that allows you to make automatic transfers.

✓ You can also cut off your monthly expenses to build the fund. For instance, consider eating home cooked meals instead of eating in the restaurant, cancel unnecessary membership subscriptions, turn down the thermostat to one or two degrees and avoid small daily purchases of discretionary items.

✓ If you have time, energy and willpower, take up a second job. Even five weeks of extra hours can make a huge difference in your fund.

✓ Sell stuff you do not need or no longer use in the house. If you look around, you will find items you can sell and get some good cash out of them. From old kids' toys, power tools, sporting equipment to extra furniture. Convert all these to cash and transfer the money to your emergency fund.

The good thing with an emergency fund is that if something goes wrong, you will be well prepared. If it goes all right instead, the money is still yours.

CREATE AN EMERGENCY MONTH EVERY YEAR

Out of the twelve months in a year, take one month and baptize it 'the emergency month.' During this month, cut down your expenses to the bare minimum and act like you have nothing, moneywise. As crazy as it may sound, it works wonders.

This month will make you understand what your priorities are and things that are just mere "wants.'

You will find yourself asking questions like, do I need to go out for dinner three times a week? Can I bring a packed lunch from home instead of eating out? Is a movie night that necessary?

The emergency month can be fun, and it allows you to save quite a good amount of money. It also helps in altering your spending habits and putting your priorities in the right order.

MAKE USE OF COUPONS AND SHOP AROUND FOR DISCOUNTS

I love using coupons , let me admit. To me, every coin counts and coupons help me save several bucks. The discounts might not be much, but they add up to quite a considerable amount. I recall one year when I saved over $4,000 with coupons. On average, the coupons saved me $80 every week.

I am also the type of person who shops around for discounts before settling on where to buy my stuff. I make good use of the internet to locate stores that are running offers, instead of going from store to store. The time and energy spent doing this is all worth it when I realize how much I have saved.

But some people hate this kind of life. I hope you are not one of them.

Some say it's a lot of work clipping the papers while others blush it off claiming it makes them look cheap. But come to think of it. if a company gives you a $20 discount for using its products, does that make you cheap? Come on!

Coupons can save you a lot of money for services you use on a regular basis. From haircuts, groceries, home services, gas and many more. You just need to be an active coupon user.

Remember not just to buy products because they are discounted. Use the coupons to purchase items you really need. Otherwise, you will not be able to make savings buying things that you do not need.

And one last thing; never be embarrassed to use coupons. Coupons are worth it, and they do not make you look cheap if used the right way.

MAIL YOUR REBATE OFFERS IMMEDIATELY AFTER PURCHASE

Just like couponing, most of us are lazy when it comes to filling out rebates. In fact, more than 60% of consumer rebates are never redeemed.

Most rebates have a turnaround of ninety days. To make the most out of your rebate, you must follow this procedure;

✓ Fill out the rebate form
✓ Provide the original receipt or a copy of the same
✓ Send your form as soon as possible

✓ Keep a copy of the form in your records for tracking via the internet in case you do not receive a rebate

To make the most out of rebates, send the forms with anything above $5.

EMBRACE A SAVING MINDSET AND DITCH THE SPENDING MINDSET

The moment you shift your mindset to saving, you will automatically become contagious to anything that helps you save. Some people say they are addicted to spending and can never change, but that is not the case. It is all in mind. They do not want to change. They love spending even when they do not have the money. They take up debts to maintain a lifestyle that then cannot afford. They lack the discipline to shift their mindset to that of 'savers.' Yet, to develop saving habits, it's a personal choice.

Our next chapter is on spending, and we shall have a chance to see how you can ditch your spending mindset once and for all.

CHAPTER 3

The Spending Lesson

"You can have a Masters degree in making money, but you will still end up broke if you have a Ph.D. in spending it."

Orrin Woodward

WHAT IS SPENDING?

Spending money simply means using the money to pay for services, personal amenities, entertainment and other activities we enjoy. Spending money is good and healthy too. After all, money is meant for spending.

There is a saying often told "Money is the root of all evil". This saying is misquoted from the holy book, The Bible. In Timothy 6:10 it states, 'For the love of money is the root of all evil.'

And now, more than two centuries later, we are advised to turn back on money because it is evil.

But is it?

We work for long hours. Put up with our demanding bosses. Get stuck in jobs we do not like but cannot resign. Play the lottery. Trade shares. Enroll in inexpensive courses to get a promotion at work and carry out all sorts of money making hustles.

We spend 6 to 7 days a week making money. Yet, we are supposed to turn our back from the 'fruits' of our labor. It's confusing, right?

But the point is, making money is good, saving it is a great idea and spending it consciously is absolutely the best idea.

Most people are extremely sold out to saving and investing, such that, they never get to enjoy their money in a way they would want. There is more to life than just saving for a rainy day.

However, most people have the habit of unconscious spending, and that is where the problem is. When you start spending out of pleasure and to please others with money that you do not have, then, just know a big problem is coming your way.

In this chapter, our focus will be on ways you can live a good life today, enjoying your money, but still be mindful of the future.

STOP KEEPING UP WITH EVERYONE ELSE.

'Keeping up with the Joneses' is an old idiom referring to how we compare ourselves to those around us to determine a particular social status. Trying to keep up with everyone puts unnecessary pressure on you to be successful, impressive and wealthy, just like those around you seem to be.

Sadly, this pressure can easily influence you to spend more money than you have, to please others. You will also accumulate credit card debts and end up buying things you do not even care about. In the long run, keeping up with the Joneses will render you broke, unhappy and eventually set back your financial goals.

It's important for you to understand that, in life, there will always be people who will live a better life than you and others who cannot afford as much as you (though their purchases might make you think otherwise.

Your goal should be to become financially responsible today so that you can progressively increase your financial position in the future.

So, how can you be true to yourself and avoid keeping up with everyone?
- ✓ Make choices that align with your values and goals in life.
- ✓ Spend on things that make you happy and not what everyone else is buying
- ✓ Get better friends and surround yourself with people who inspire and support you and keep away from those who put unnecessary pressure on you
- ✓ Learn to live within your means

HOW TO SPEND WITHIN YOUR MEANS (WITHOUT FEELING LIMITED)

Can you imagine going to a birthday party while dieting? You get to salivate at the sight of piles of cheese, dessert platters and an open bar. Your friends are enjoying every morsel of indulgence and the temptation to join in is overwhelming.

Well, depending on your willpower you may just fall for the temptation. However, if you are fully dedicated to your dieting mission, the temptation will not weigh you a single inch.

Why did I give this as an example?

This is exactly what happens when you are required to spend within your means. Sometimes it feels restrictive and limiting your life. The feeling that you want a good life but you do not have enough can easily result in poorer financial decision making.

So, what do you do when you feel financially limited? Below are four strategies you can implement to start spending within your means, without the detrimental feeling of limitation.

Strategy #1:   Get creative with the recurring expenses

Comb through your list of expenses and find out how you can adjust them without making major lifestyle alterations. Identify what you can renegotiate or replace with alternatives that fit within your budget. For example, you can call up your internet provider and negotiate for a better rate. You can also try finding out what options their competitors have.

Strategy #2:   Spread out the splurges

Splurges are cool. It's a way of treating our bodies and paying ourselves for all the hard work. However, frequent splurges are not good for our financial security. Spreading them out is a good way of making sure we do not dispose them off. For instance, if you indulge in a spa treatment every month, you can try and schedule it on a quarterly basis. A manicure can also wait for a month, instead of having it weekly (unless your nails chip badly)

Strategy #3:   Learn to shop smart

Always compare prices before paying for an item or service. Researching price ranges of different brands and stores can help you land great deals for the very same items. You can also try asking for a discount every time you are shopping. Most stores do not have fixed prices for their items, and there is always room for negotiations. Inquiries will not only help you pay less, but they also ensure you are living within your means. Remember to never feel embarrassed for your queries. After all, you are the one paying for the bills and not anyone else.

Strategy #4:   Of course, make more money

If you do not want to feel restricted or cheap, then you need to earn more. Making more money will not only help you spend comfortably, but it will also allow you to fatten your savings account. You can create a side hustle or take up a second job to make more money. This will ease the feeling of limitation and struggles that might squeeze you way beyond living within your means.

HOW TO TRIM YOUR EXPENSES EFFORTLESSLY

When you are living on a budget, trimming your expenses is a no-brainer. It's something you must to do. The good thing is that you can still manage to cut down your household expenses with little effort.

Trimming Food Expenses

Tip #1:   Buy in bulk when stuff is on sale

We all go crazy when foodstuffs are on sale. Try to make use of sales by buying non-perishable items in bulk. However, be careful not to buy too much as they may end up expiring before usage.

Tip #2:   Compare prices

Grocery prices vary from one store to another. One store could be selling veggies at a cheap price while another stocks cereals at low prices. Compare prices to ascertain where to get items at a much lower cost.

Tip #3:   Plan meals in advance

You are probably wondering what a meal plan has to do with trimming your expenses. When you plan your meals for a week or two, it makes it easy to build a grocery list. It also makes it easy for you to plan the grocery and avoid regular impulse buying of items, you probably do not need.

Tip #4:   Avoid buying already prepared foods

Whenever possible, make your food from scratch. Although pre-prepared foods offload the headache of food preparation, they tend to be more expensive. The next time you go to the stores, be sure to compare prices of a ready to eat lasagna vs. making one at home, or ready to eat salad vs. preparing one from scratch. The ready to eat tend to be way too expensive. Cooking from scratch might seem too much work. However, if you make use of a few tricks like using a slow cooker, cooking in bulk and making one-pot meals, you will fall in love with this saving trick.

Trimming Clothing Expenses

Tip #1:   If you don't need it, don't buy it

If only everyone were loyal to this rule, saving accounts would never run dry. Make an effort to only buy new clothes when replacing those that have worn out. You will be amazed at how little you will be spending on clothing if you avoid impulse buying and instead only purchase clothes when necessary.

Tip #2:   Consider second hand and thrift stores

These stores are way cheaper compared to outlets that deal with new clothing. The good thing is that you can get quality apparel at thrift stores, at unbelievably low prices.

Tip #3:   Buy out of season whenever possible

At the end of every season, most clothing is marked down to rock–bottom prices. Take advantage of the opportunity to buy stuff you need. Over the long term, this will save you tons of money.

Tip #4:   If you only need it once, then borrow it

Sometimes, we need a special outfit for certain occasions. However, some of these outfits can only be worn once and never again. To save on this, ask around and see if someone or an outlet can lend you the outfit you need. It is much cheaper.

Tip #5:   Avoid clothing that needs dry cleaning

If possible, stick to machine washable clothing. Clothes that require dry cleaning will see you spend too much money every time you need them cleaned.

Trimming Healthcare Costs

Tip #1:   Prevention is better than cure

Preventing diseases is the best way to cut down on healthcare costs. You can do this by exercising regularly, eating healthy and maintaining a healthy weight.

Tip #2:   Make use of coupons and discounts

Some manufacturers provide doctors with coupons for expensive brand name medication. If you are under a costly prescription, ask your doctor if such coupons are available (or when they will be available) to help chop the medication price.

Tip #3:   Ask for a less expensive generic medication

People often mistake generic medicine for imitations. But that isn't so. In the medication world, the active ingredient is what makes the difference. According to law, any medication must have a specific amount of the active ingredient. Therefore, most licensed medicines are the same; it's only the names that are different. In fact, your body might not even notice the difference between generic and brand names, but your bank account surely will.

Tip #4:   Stick to providers within your insurance

Insurance companies often partner with different medical providers for competitive rates. If you go outside the partners within the insurance company, you will be required to pay extra money, if the difference in cost ends up being more expensive.

Tip #5:   Always compare prices

Let's say you need surgery. The cost can vary widely depending on the facility you check into. The most important thing is to check the prices of the surgery, lab work and diagnostic tests for different facilities.

Trimming Household and Cleaning Supplies

Tip #1:   Switch to fluorescent light bulbs

Although expensive in the short term, fluorescent light bulbs last much longer. They also consume less energy than the regular bulbs thus saving you much money in the long run.

Tip #2:   Whenever possible, use store brands

For instance, when buying sugar, opt for the generic store brand of your retail shop other than the re-known brand names. The store brands are not only just the same as the expensive brand, but you will also get them at a much lower price.

Tip #3:   Opt for multipurpose and reusable supplies

Choose items that can be used for an array of purposes. For instance, instead of using paper towels to dust counter tops, get a washable rug that you can reuse over and over again. Also, instead of using a separate cleaner for every single surface, choose a multipurpose cleaner instead.

Tip #4:   Make good use of homemade cleaning solutions

Did you know that a mixture of vinegar and water is an ultimate cleaner for hard floors? Baking soda also works great as an abrasive cleaner. There are hundreds of cheap homemade cleaning solutions that you can always adopt instead of buying expensive detergents and cleansers.

UNDERSTANDING AND TRANSFORMING YOUR SPENDING HABIT

A habit is an acquired behavior usually followed regularly. Some people have good spending habits while others have spending habits that could best be termed as unhealthy. Separating some of your bad spending habits from the good ones is not always easy.

Spending habits could include anything from spending lots of money as soon as you receive your pay, waiting until the last minute to buy a plane ticket or even donating 10% of your paycheck to a charity.

Our strong habits are formed and influenced mainly by those around us. This includes;

- ✓ **Spiritual beliefs;** religion impacts our spending habits in the aspects of tithing, giving alms, giving to charity and celebrations that require certain expenses to be met
- ✓ **Culture and society;** someone who has been brought up in a wealthy family, will have an entirely different spending habit from that of someone raised in a poor environment. Similarly, a person from the Asian culture might have no problem spending lavishly on weddings compared to a person from a culture that does not have much enthusiasm for weddings.
- ✓ **Parents and guardians;** if you grew up around people who always bought flowers when visiting relatives, you might find yourself following a similar trend whenever appropriate.

Breaking spending habits is very difficult. Over time, the habit becomes more and more natural to us. And according to research, we will always tend to favor what is familiar with us even if we know it's not to our benefit. However, it does not mean that spending habits cannot be changed. The challenge is creating a new behavior pattern that will ultimately lead to behavior change.

To achieve this, you will need to ask yourself these questions, as they will help sort out your good spending habits from the bad ones.

Question #1: Is it aligned with the important things in your life?

Most of the time, we find ourselves spending on things that add little or no value in our life- just out of a pure habit. We also tend to purchase stuff to keep up with our friends or to settle an internal battle of compare and despair.

Before purchasing an item, always ask yourself this one question. Is this item aligned with the important things in my life? If you have well-stipulated values, a clear life purpose and a laid-out focus in life, it'll be impossible to splurge your money on a lifestyle that does not fit with your values.

If you get into the habit of spending your hard-earned money on the things you value, it can hugely enhance your life.

Question #2: Is it helping you build wealth?

Building up wealth isn't always a walk in the park. It calls for sacrifice, and the journey is not always a pleasant one. For instance, saving up to pay your student loans instead of saving for a vacation can feel like you are entering snooze. But come to think of it. In the long run, paying the student loans will enable you to build your wealth in the future. So, if something is not helping you accumulate wealth, think twice before spending on it.

Question #3: Does it make you happy?

Some purchases give us a quick thrill, but others spark happiness in our lives forever. In most cases, stuff bought on impulse boost our psyche for a moment but later leave us with a feeling of remorse.

Always take time to figure out if an item is worth spending money on. The purchase should add an overall well-being to you (for a long time not temporal.) If you are not sure about it, give yourself some breathing room to seek clarity.

Remember that what tickles another person's heart could be freaking to you. A curio collector will be thrilled by making purchases of rare trinkets, while an outdoor adventure person is amazed by backpacking accessories.

So, spend money on what you genuinely love, and this will enable you to focus on things that will always spark happiness in your life.

LEARN TO PRIORITIZE YOUR SPENDING

You will agree with me that it is impossible to have it all in life. Even billionaires do not have everything they would wish to have. Sometimes you will find yourself having to choose between dinner out and credit card debt. Or building an emergency fund and providing opportunities for your children.

The truth is that prioritizing your spending is very hard, but when done right, it can literally pay off. When you determine what your priorities in life are, it's easy to shift your financial resources into that direction without feeling a pinch in your bank account.

The ultimate way to prioritize on spending is to define your needs and wants.

What are needs?

Needs are paramount for survival. They are the items we need to survive. They include basic amenities such as food, clothing, shelter and a way to make money to meet our living expenses is also a need. Entertainment, transportation, insurance costs, and utility bill payments are also part of our living arrangements.

What are wants?

What we want makes our lives more enjoyable. In most cases, they are an extension of our needs. We can live without these things, but life will not be as fun. For instance, though food is a need, eating out is a want. A shelter is a need, but when you determine how big you want an apartment to be, this is a want. Nice cars and beautiful clothing are also wants extended from our needs.

Verdict

Needs should always be prioritized. However, some wants can also be prioritized depending on what you consider important in life and what you want your money to accomplish.

If you think paying off your student loans is an important thing, then you will have to trade it with something else. For instance, you might stop paying for the monthly cable TV if you feel that it is hindering your efforts to pay off the debt.

Likewise, if socializing is an important aspect to you, then add a few dollars in your budget to cater for social events and eating out. On the other hand, if you fancy a home entertainment system, then prioritize on a large screen TV to serve the purpose. You can also invest in a nice car but then consider downsizing on the size of your apartment.

Remember that, you can never have it all. You must prioritize some things at the expense of others that you will need to trade off.

IDENTIFY AND PAY ALL BILLS ON TIME (AND KEEP ALL THE RECEIPTS)

If you get into the habit of paying up what you owe on time, it will prevent you from developing money management problems. Paying your bills late attracts interest charges that can be avoided if you are not too lazy to mail their payments in good time. Some companies even cut off their services and demand for a reconnection fee when on-time payments are not made.

As you pay the bills, also remember to pay the government in good time. Pay the property taxes, state taxes, automobile registrations and every other fee that you owe the government. There is no need to get into legal trouble for ignoring or delaying the government financial obligations.

Most importantly, review and keep the receipts. The receipts come in handy when you need proof for warranty or guarantee in the instance an appliance breaks down. Instead of buying a new one, with the receipt in hand, you will get a new one (or servicing) for free.

CHAPTER 4

The Investing Lesson

"Poor people see a dollar as a dollar to trade for something they want right now. Rich people see every dollar as a 'seed' that can be planted to earn a hundred more dollars ... then replanted to earn a thousand more dollars."

Harv Eker

WHAT IS INVESTING?

Investing is a way of committing money to a project with the expectation of it obtaining profit. Investing should allow us to work smarter and not harder. For instance, when we work hard and for long hours, putting some of our earnings towards our future needs is an intelligent way of investing.

Investment is, therefore, money that you have set aside to work for you while you are busy with life. This way, you can reap happily when the harvest time comes. Investing is also a means to a happy ending that requires you to prioritize your financial future over your present desires.

HOW IS INVESTMENT DIFFERENT FROM SAVING?

Some people use these two terms interchangeably, yet they are entirely different concepts. Each of these financial strategies leads to a very different outcome from the other.

Savings can be seen as a short-term goal of up to three years. For instance, you can save towards a holiday shopping, vacation or a new car. Saving requires you to keep the money in a safe place where you can easily retrieve it when you need it. Saving earns you interest but not as much as what investment can make you.

Investing, on the other hand, involves putting up money for a bigger long-term goal of more than five years. Investments require more money, and you invest with the hope that over time, it will generate returns. Unlike savings, investments are risky; in fact, the more you want to invest the more the risk involved.

The most attractive long-term investment options are buying assets such as mutual funds, stocks, bonds, and real estate. Building your retirement fund and saving for your child's college education can also be categorized as a form of investment.

TRY TO KEEP OFF GET RICH QUICK SCAMS

It's unfortunate that unscrupulous financial advisors are putting the savings of thousands of people at risk by encouraging them to invest in schemes destined to 'make them get rich fast.' Unfortunately, the only people who benefit from these schemes are those marketing and advocating for them.

Innocent savers are conned every day by cold callers posing as financial gurus claiming to make money grow fast in dodgy investments. These schemes promise extremely high profits for a relatively small investment of time and money. If you are sensible enough, you will stay away from them, since they always sound too good to be true.

Some examples of these schemes include
- ✓ **The Advance fee fraud**; the scammers will often ask you for up-front fees on the basis that, the fees are payments to authorize huge sums of money
- ✓ **Pyramid schemes**; here, you are urged to recruit members with a promise of payments for enrolling others. You are made to believe that, your work is not to sell products but to get more people selling underneath you
- ✓ **Infomercials**; while some infomercials are genuine, avoid those that show people making plenty of money using a too-good-to-be-true strategy
- ✓ **Ponzi schemes**; these fraud schemes work on the premise of 'robbing Peter to pay Paul.' The scheme promises its members high returns with little or no risks involved. Ponzi generates returns for old investors by acquiring

new members. The problem arises when you need your principal back, and they take you in circles.

✓ Work at home schemes that make millions; if it were true, everyone would quit their jobs to work from home. This scheme often requires you to purchase a product and market it. Ultimately, this ends up becoming a total waste of money.

✓ Pitches that sell a secret formula; avoid these schemes since they are fraud. Nothing is a secret in the internet world anymore. If indeed that formula is thriving as the scheme dictates, then everyone would be aware of it already.

The thing is; if something sounds too sweet to be true, keep off it and run away. The best way to get rich in life is by working smarter but not by taking shortcuts.

TYPES OF INVESTMENTS

Investments are tools that help us achieve our financial goals. There are many types of investments, but in our case, we are only going to look at the most common.

Type #1: Stocks

When a company wants to expand, but there is no enough funds to do this, they turn to the financial market. The company is then split into shares, and a portion of it sold in the open market in a process known as IPO.

When you purchase shares of a company, you own a piece of that company's stock. Stocks then make you part of the company no matter how small your shares are. From time to time, the company pays dividends to its owners.

Type #2: Bonds

Bonds represent debt. A government or corporation might need money to expand but has none or does not have enough. The institutions then borrow money in the financial market with the promise of paying it at a specified date. Therefore, bonds can be defined as a loan investors make to institutions, in exchange for interest payments over a given time, plus repayment of the principal amount at the bond's maturity date.

Type #3: Mutual Funds

Mutual funds pool your money together with that of other investors to purchase shares, bonds, and other securities. Mutual funds are ideal for regular investors who do not know much about investing.

Type #4: Bank products

Banks and credit unions provide safe and convenient ways for investors to accumulate savings. These could include checking and savings accounts that offer not only liquidity but also flexibility.

Type #5:   Annuities

An agreement between you and an insurance company where they promise to be making periodic payments is called an annuity. The payments can start immediately or at some future time.

Type #6:   Retirement

Numerous investment options come into play when saving for retirement and managing it once you retire. For purposes of saving, tax advantage retirement options or IRAs, can be a smart choice for your retirement plan investment.

Type #7:   Saving for college

Funding college begins with savings. You, therefore, need to learn various smart ways to save and plan for your children's college fees.

Others:

Type #8:   Commodity features

Type #9:   Security features

Type #10: Insurance

Type #11: Cryptocurrencies

DIVERSIFYING YOUR INVESTMENT PORTFOLIO

Diversifying is another way of saying 'don't put all your eggs in one basket.' Diversifying means spreading your assets in a variety of investments. Doing this protects you from a huge setback in case of risks.

A smart investor does not invest all his money in buying a single type of investment like stocks. Instead, his portfolio comprises of a mix of investments such as stocks, bonds, mutual funds, real estate, commodities among others.

Some people don't like investing in stocks and bonds at the same time. However, the advantage of investing in both is because they tend to do the opposite of each other. For instance, when stocks are doing well, the bonds tend to be on the low side and vice versa. Therefore, your money is working for you at all times, and this minimizes your risk of losing everything at the same time.

IF POSSIBLE, AVOID INVESTING WITH FAMILY AND FRIENDS

The fastest way to break relationships with loved ones is by investing with family and friends. Well, I am not insinuating that all investments done with them will turn out badly, but the truth is that most of them do.

We trust our friends and family members so much that, we can easily invest and loan them hundreds of dollars without getting anything in writing. We get reluctant hiring a lawyer because we trust them and taking a legal measure can potentially make the relationship uncomfortable.

Suing people who share a strong bond with you because they failed to fulfill their part of the bargain is never an easy thing. It breaks relationships, family reunions, church functions, neighborhood spirit and generally makes everything you share uncomfortable. So, before you decide to follow your gut and do business with these people, think about this ugly feeling.

On the other hand, investing with people who are not very close to you has many advantages. First, it takes emotion out of the equation thus helping you focus on the merits of the opportunity you are eyeing. In the case where things end up getting nasty, you will be comfortable taking the matter to court to protect your interests.

It, however, doesn't mean that all investments done with friends and family are destined to fail. Here are a few tips to make it successful

- ✓ From the beginning, make it clear that you are considering both the best and the worst case scenarios for the partnership. In the case, things go south, emphasize that seeking legal help will be your ultimate path.
- ✓ Be diligent with documents from the initial stages. Some people use minimal documents with the people they trust, and this ends up ruining their investments
- ✓ Beware of scenarios where you are needed as a guarantor, requests for secrecy and instances where someone needs urgent money. Be sure to ask hard questions before giving in.
- ✓ When investing with friends, let them know that you made a promise to your spouse or parents that you would always use an Attorney when you put your money in investments.

The point is that, if you feel thorough documentation, suing and asking hard question is not something you would like to do, then avoid investing with family and friends.

CHAPTER 5

The Debt Lesson
'Debts are nowadays like children; begot with pleasure,but brought forth in pain.'
Moliere

WHAT IS DEBT?

A debt is an amount of money that you owe another person or an organization that loaned you. Debts accrue interest charges which are termed as additional costs for the privilege. Debts can be as big as your mortgage and student loan or as small as a bank draft or $20 that a friend lends you. Just like fat, debts are easy to accumulate but hard to eliminate.

In these modern times, it's nearly impossible to live a debt free life. Most of us cannot afford to buy homes or pay for college fees from the pocket. Borrowing money hence comes in handy to help us achieve these things in life.

The most important thing however, is to take debts in moderation. You should also only take debts that work for you and not against you. Below, we shall have a look at the differences between good and bad debts.

GOOD DEBT VS. BAD DEBTS

Basically, there is no form of debt that is inherently good. However, some debts are not as bad, since they contribute to our financial future in meaningful ways. Understanding the difference between good and bad debts will help you determine which form you should pay first, and the one that you should avoid entirely for your stability and peace of mind.

WHAT IS GOOD DEBT?

Just as the name suggests, this type of debt is not badly off. A good debt contributes to your financial future and it helps in generating long term income. When you take a loan to manage your finances, secure your future, invest in yourself or to consolidate debt, then this type of debt is worth it. Although the debt will initially put a dent in your wallet, it will be worth it in the long run.

Examples of good debts include;

Mortgage

A mortgage has two advantages. First, you get a place to live and second, you live in a place that gains value every year. That means that, if you will ever think of selling your home in future, your bank account will be smiling all the way.

For instance, if you buy a home for $235,000 and it appreciates 3% every year, this means that it will be worth $485,000 by the time your 30-year mortgage is paid off.

Indeed, that's a good debt.

Student Loans

Most of us want a good education, but in most cases, we cannot afford it. The student loan industry is expanding very first with Americans carrying a total of $1.4 trillion as student loan debt.

A student loan is worth it, only if you are investing in an education that will lead to a well- paying career. Getting into a career that will pay you less than $30,000 a year is not worth taking a loan for. With all the expenses and tough economic times we are currently living in, you will find it very hard paying your debt.

Home Equity Loans

These loans have very low interest rates and the lending companies use your home as collateral. Home equity loans are great if you want to pay off a higher interest debt or make essential home improvements that will increase the value of your home.

WHAT IS BAD DEBT?

When I was 19, I went to Sears and my credit card was approved. I was starting a life away from my parents, and there was no way I would make it boring. I immediately bought a couch, fancy lamp and an answering machine.

Before, I even paid the debt in full, there was nothing to show for it. The couch was ripped, the lamp broken and the answering machine no longer functioned. To make it worse, I still had a bill for items I no longer used.

That was definitely a bad debt.

A bad debt is one used to purchase items that quickly lose value leaving you with nothing to show for it. Most forms of bad debts are offered by non-financial institutions that charge exorbitantly high interest rates.

Examples of Bad ebt

Credit Card Debt

Over 121 million Americans have credit card debt making it the most pervasive form of bad debt in the US. On average, credit card debt per person amounts to $4,453.

Credit cards are created for convenience. The cards also have lots of consumer perks in the form of points and rewards. However, they are categorized as bad debt because of their high interest rate.

For instance, you can swipe your card to buy a $1,200 TV screen at 18.9% interest rate. If you are required to pay $60 per month, it would take you 63 months to pay off the debt that would cost you a total of $1,676. That is a hefty interest of over $400 being paid to a credit company for the privilege of using their card.

Pay Day Loans

Just like credit cards, pay day loans are equally terrible. Sometimes even worse. You get a short-term loan to get through a crisis and promise to pay the cash when your paycheck arrives.

Payday loans accrue exorbitant interest rates and repayment requirements are immediate, when you receive a paycheck. Failure to pay the principal amount, plus the interest charges accrues another processing fee to roll over to your loan.

Since the loan is paid within a short term, you might not feel the impact as the borrower. But come to think of it; if you are charged the rate of 30% for every $100 borrowed that is a whopping annual rate of 400%.

If that doesn't make you ditch pay day loans, then you need to see a financial advisor.

Auto Loans

Car loans can be good or bad. Sometimes, a car can be a necessity and that taking a loan for its purchase becomes a worth venture. However, if you are taking a car loan to keep up with the Joneses, then it's a bad idea.

Sadly, most people take higher car loans than they can afford. They end up paying for a car that is no longer running or they are not even investing in anymore.

EASY WAYS TO ELIMINATE DEBT IN YOUR LIFE

To get out of debt, you need to pay it off. However, the process is not as easy as it sounds. In the current climate, credit companies are mushrooming every day and you can easily find yourself tangled in huge amounts of debt.

If you are already swimming in debt and not sure how to get out of it, you are not alone. On average, every US household has a nearly $17,000 credit card debt.

Below are some best strategies and easy ways that will get you started in paying off that debt.

Strategy #1:   Create a Budget

There is no need to expound on this. The first chapter of this covers everything that will enable you create a workable budget. Be sure to check it out.

Strategy #2:   Pay more than the minimum balance

By paying more than your minimum balance on your credit card, you prolong a debt pay off strategy. You can further strengthen your commitment to pay off by making small weekly payments instead of monthly payments. Another trick would be to double your payments. For instance, if your minimal payment is $100 try making it $200 or more.

Strategy #3:   Put bonuses towards debt

Although we had discussed it earlier, bonuses can be unexpected and you can easily misuse them. If you receive a bonus, use it to pay a debt and avoid the temptation to purchase discretionary items. It will be worth it fixing your financial situation, than owning the latest designer bag in the long run.

Strategy #4:   Delete credit card information from online stores

If you are an online shopping enthusiast, it's likely that you have stored your credit card information on several sites. While that makes the checkout process easier, it also makes it quicker to buy items you do not need. So, get rid of that information. Instead, make use of a debit card.

Strategy #5:   Sell stuff to settle the debt

Search through your home and look out for stuff you can sell. eBay and Craigslist are good platforms to sell the items faster. Just make sure you take quality photos, enter attention grabbing captions and reasonable prices.

Strategy #6: Change your habits

Your untamed spending habits got you into this mess. Spend some time to figure out how to tame them. In Chapter 3 we looked at various ways that you can change your habits to reach your financial goal.

Strategy #7: Reward yourself when you finally reach the milestone

The fastest way to pay off a debt is to view it as a motivation and not a punishment. When you finally get yourself out of the bondage, reward your hard work. Remember not to take out another debt, in order to pay yourself. If you do, you are just setting back your financial goals.

DEBUNKING THE MOST COMMON DEBT MYTHS

Myths can be popular but they are built on a weak foundation of false information. Money and debt topics can be confusing, especially with contradicting opinions and myths floating around us.

A basic understanding of debt myths and truths is paramount to help you make the best decision regarding your financial well-being.

Myth #1: Credit cards from favorite retailers are the best

Pitches from your favorite retail store can sound enticing. From interest free financing and other rewards, but if you carry a balance to the next month, the deals are not as appealing.

Most of these cards allow you to purchase items on credit but then pay them off within a given period at no interest. However, if you fail to pay within that time, your interest is calculated for the entire amount you initially owed. In most cases, the interest you will be charged is higher than what you would have paid for a regular credit card.

Myth#2: Marriage makes you responsible for your spouse's debt

It's not the case. Marriage does not mandate you to pay off a debt your spouse incurred before marriage. However, if you refinance a loan with your spouse, put your name on a loan's promissory note or become a joint holder of a credit card, you will likely become responsible for those debts.

Myth #3:   Joint debts are separated after divorce

A divorce decree can help separate marital debts but not joint debts. Your lender has no idea about your divorce and therefore your agreement remains. The best thing would be talk to your lender and discuss about the divorce decree. Where possible, he will offer options available.

Myth #4:   Bankruptcy is the only option to pay off massive debt

Bankruptcy is not the only option available to pay off large debts. You can involve a financial advisor to advise on other debt management plans and relief options available.

Myth #4:   You are too rich to qualify for student loans

Some well off families shy off from student loans for the mere mentality that they do not qualify. As a result, they turn to private loans which charge exorbitant rates. It's important to note that most federal loans have no income limits and therefore encourage all society classes to apply.

Myth #5:   If I loan money to loved ones, I am helping them

The truth is that, you are saving their financial crisis but that will strain and destroy your relationship. I want to believe that you have loaned money to a friend,only for them to never reply to your calls again. If you must give friends and relatives money, consider it a gift. If they refund it, well and good; If they do not, then you have no grudges whatsoever.

Myth #6:   Debt is a tool to create prosperity

Although we have been made to believe that debt is a tool that will make us rich, it is not always true. Debts bring risk to our lives and this has the ability of offsetting any benefits, that could have been gained through leverage of debt.

Myth #7:   Lotto and gambling will make you rich

Gambling is a tax on the poor people who are lazy to do the math. Rich and smart people never play these games. They clearly understand that these are rip-off institutions and not wealth building tools as we are meant to believe. Wealth is built on energy, diligence and thrift, but not on dumb luck of false hope and denial.

SMART WAYS TO USE CREDIT CARDS THE RIGHT WAY

Whether you have been using credit cards for many years, or you are just getting started, they can be confusing. Depending on your discipline to use them, they can turn out incredibly dangerous or immensely helpful.

To make the most of your card and to avoid dismissing your credit card altogether, adopt these small habits that will help you unlock the benefits the right way.

Smart tip #1: Set a sensible credit card limit

Your credit card limit should be an amount you can repay comfortably. It needs to be an amount that will not tempt you to spend more than you can afford. If you cannot afford to pay off your balance every month, do not raise the limit. A higher limit will tempt you to easily get into more debt.

Smart tip #2: Reduce your credit card limit

It might sound crazy, but it's a smart idea. Reducing the limit will help you avoid the temptation to get into credit card debt. You can either do it online or make a request to your credit card provider to reduce the credit limit.

Smart tip #3: Always pay your bill in full (and never late)

Never carry a balance to the next month if you don't want to end up like the average American. Paying your bill on time avoids being charged with interest and helps you build a high credit score. Believe me, a 50% off sale means nothing when you get slapped with an 18% interest charge.

Smart tip #4: Keep in mind your credit card payment date

If you have a problem remembering your credit card payment date, pick a date that easily sticks in your head. Better still, set a reminder on your phone a few days before the due date. Another option would be to authorize an automatic transfer to pay the bill through a direct bank draft.

Smart tip #5: Use your card only for big stuff

Most people who get into credit card debt are regular buyers of small purchases that end up becoming huge amounts if left unchecked.

The best way is to use your card for big purchases only. A great idea is to save up for your item in cash first. Then make your purchase and after reaping the reward points, you can now top up your credit card.

Smart tip #6: Opt for cards with extra perks

Besides reward points, some credit cards out there have extra benefits such as price protection, extended warranties, free travel insurance and rental car coverage.

However, you only get to enjoy these benefits if you pay your balance in full every month. So, do your research to determine the companies with these types of cards.

Smart tip #7: Don't use credit cards to make ends meet

If you are running low on cash or an emergency happens, avoid using your credit card to get out of the mess. It might save you for the immediate crisis, but over time you will end up getting into debt. As for emergencies, learn how to build an emergency fund, see Chapter 2 of this book.

CHAPTER 6

The Insurance Lesson

"At the same cost spent on occasional pizzas or dine outs, one can cover premium costs - for lasting protection - with insurance."

Meera Srinivasan

WHAT IS INSURANCE?

Insurance is a contract where an individual or entity receives financial protection against losses from an insurance company. Insurance protects you from financial loss in the case where things go wrong.

However, while insurance can grant you peace of mind, it is not like a savings account, where every single coin you pay belongs to you. In insurance, the only money you can claim back depends on what your insurance contract covers.

IMPORTANT TERMS ABOUT INSURANCE

Annuity
The agreement by an insurer to make periodic payments over a specified period.
Policyholder
A person who owns the insurance policy.
Risk
The condition where there is a possibility of loss from an event that cannot be entirely controlled. The term is also used for the person or property insured.
Premium

A specified amount payable by the insured person for the coverage of the expectation of loss.

Co-Insurance
Here, the insured individual is required to pay a certain percentage of a loss after the deductible is paid.
Liability
The condition of being bound by the insurance policy to do something that may be enforced in the courts.
Endorsements
Modifications made to an insurance policy to meet special needs of an individual risk.
Agent
A person by the state insurance authority to sell insurance products.
Underwriting
The process where an insurance company examines a risk and determines who will be offered an insurance policy and at what price.
Policy
The contract that states the terms of the insurance like the risks covered and amount payable in the case of losses.
Beneficiary
The person who receives money in the case where an insured person passes on.
Claim
This is a formal request the policyholder makes to the insurance company asking for payment after the occurrence of an accident, injury or illness.
Coverage
The types of risks covered by an insurance policy as well as the amount of money to be paid in the case of losses.
Deductible
The out of pocket money a policy holder usually pays before the insurance company covers the remaining costs attributed to a loss.
Dependent
The person who relies on someone else for care.

TYPES OF INSURANCE YOU NEED (AND POLICIES YOU DO NOT NEED)

Insurance can protect you but it can seem like a huge waste of resources, if the policy is not something you need. On the other hand, if you find yourself in a serious problem, not having insurance can turn the situation into a financial catastrophe.

It is therefore essential to recognize the insurance policies which are the most important to protecting you and can be easily incorporated into your budget.

POLICIES YOU SHOULD NOT GO WITHOUT

Life Insurance

According to the Insurance Information Institute, only 70% of Americans have a life insurance cover.

Many people take life insurance too lightly. Others consider it important to the married people or those with children. However, life insurance is for everyone since it meets several financial needs.

If you were to pass away unexpectedly, how would your family pay for monthly expenses? (especially if you were the bread winner) your spouse, children or parents should not be left behind worrying, how to survive financially in your absence.

With a life insurance that provides up to 12 times your yearly income, your family will not be worried about making ends meet, losing their home or change of college plans.

Remember that, the younger you are, the more affordable life insurance is. So, there is no reason why as a single person, with no dependent, should not take a cover.

Auto Insurance

Driving around uninsured is not only against the law, but losing an uninsured car in an accident can be quite hectic. In the case where the accident is your fault, the liability on your shoulder could end up becoming very expensive. Auto insurance comes with various options that you can choose from.

- ✓ **Liability Coverage**;   if you are at fault in an accident, this coverage takes care of all the costs relating to injuries and property damage.

✓ **Collision coverage;** this covers any costs related to repair or replacement of your damaged car

✓ **Comprehensive coverage;** the comprehensive cover takes care of your losses that are not caused by an accident. This could include theft, vandalism, flood, fire and hail.

Homeowners and /or Renters Insurance

As you insure your home, ensure that the policy includes an extended dwelling coverage. This way, the insurance company will rebuild your home even when the cost exceeds your coverage. It's also important to check with your company whether the aspects listed below are covered in your policy.

✓ **Flood insurance** – most policies do not cover the flood insurance. This insurance is also different from water backup protection. Therefore, talk to your agent over the details of your policy.

✓ **Earthquake coverage**- depending on where you live, your policy might exclude the earthquake insurance. Therefore, check with your insurance company for vivid details.

As a renter, do not undermine the importance of getting renters insurance. Without it, it means that you will have to personally replace your belongings in case of fire, flood, burglary and other types of disasters. Paying that kind of money out of your pocket can be very overwhelming.

Health Insurance

Good health allows you to work, earn a living and enjoy life. If you develop a serious illness or get involved in an accident when you are not insured, you might find yourself sinking into debt as you seek treatment. Luckily, most employers provide medical insurance benefits to their employees.

However, if you are self-employed or your employer does not offer such a medical cover, you will need to explore other health care insurance options.

Not having a health insurance is like gambling your life. A healthy person accumulates thousands of dollars as health costs annually. If you have a chronic disease or need regular hospitalization, the costs can run up to six figures.

Indeed, not having a health insurance can both be a physical and financial nightmare. Ensure you are well covered to avoid leaving yourself on the financial end.

Long Term Care Insurance

Long term care insurance covers services like nursing home care and other in-home help services like grooming, eating and bathing. Basically, long term care insurance is the ongoing assistance for the aged, people living with disability or chronic illnesses.

Your health insurance policy will not cover for long term care expenses given that they are very expensive.

The best time to purchase a long-term care insurance would be a day before you are going to need it. Unfortunately, you can never be sure when that day will be. Therefore, the ideal period to get the cover is between the age of 50 and 60. The price of the cover also goes up as the insured gets older. The coverage is also not available for senior citizens over the age of 80.

Identity Theft Protection

According to a 2017 study released by Javelin Strategy and Research, identity thieves stole over $16 billion from about 15 million consumers in the US. No matter how careful you are, cyber-crime and identity fraud are real threats to our personal information. Hackers constantly attack the payment systems of retail stores leaving millions of people vulnerable to theft.

Cleaning up an identity fraud mess can take decades to handle on your own. However, with identity theft insurance, a qualified counselor is assigned the task to clean up the mess for you.

Long Term Disability Insurance

In the case where you are unable to work for a long period due to an illness or injury, long term disability insurance protects you from loss of income. Since no one knows when disability can hit, it's important to take the insurance when you are still young.

Fortunately, most employers offer long term disability insurance to their employees.

POLICES YOU DO NOT NEED

Life Insurance for Your Children

The sole purpose of life insurance is to provide for your family in the case of your premature death. Considering that your children are most likely not contributing financially to the family's well-being, you will be better off skipping this cover. The only exception is when your child (ren) earns a significant income that contributes to the family's welfare.

Mortgage Life Insurance

Basiclally, this insurance will pay off your mortgage in the case of your death. If It seems like a very reasonable policy, it will relieve your family the headache during that grieving time.

However, if you already have a term life insurance, then there is no need to have mortgage life insurance. A good life insurance will provide your family with enough money to handle the mortgage and other bills.

Cancer and Other Disease Insurance

Most health policies have dents in their coverage. For this reason, specific disease insurance policies have become popular in recent years.

The problem with these policies is that, they are very specific and most cases do not cover every detail related to the diseases. For instance, cancer insurance policies cover specific conditions and skin cancers is not among them. Yet, skin cancer is the most common form of the disease.

Instead of putting your money into a specific disease insurance policy, it would be better to upgrade your current health insurance. This way, you will be assured of being covered no matter what happens.

Credit Card Insurance

If you are the type of person that constantly carries a balance on your credit card, having a policy that will cater for the bill in the event you are unable to do so may seem like a smart plan.

But come to think of it. You will be paying monthly premiums only to have your benefits capped and still remain in debt.

It is more reasonable to send this amount towards your bill to get the balance paid off. This way, you will not only save money on interest but also avoid having to pay another bill.

CHAPTER 7

The Housing Lesson

If you rent, the rent goes up every year. But if you buy a 30-year mortgage, the cost is fixed.

John Paulson

WHAT IS HOUSING?

A house is one of the biggest things you can ever purchase in your life. However, choosing your ideal home can be exciting and terrifying at the same time. You will need to decide, if you want to rent, buy or take a mortgage.

When you think about owning a home, there are many considerations that you need to make. Such include;
- ✓ How long do you plan to stay in that house
- ✓ Do you have enough money to own a house
- ✓ If you intend to take a loan, can you afford to repay the monthly installments stress free?

Below, we shall discuss three housing options in detail, to help you choose the best choice that fits you.

THE RENTING LESSON

There are many misconceptions about renting a home. We are discouraged from renting because it's a way of making your landlord richer instead of yourself. We have been made to believe that renting is like throwing money away.

However, there is much about renting that is left unearthed. For this reason, let's uncover some of the considerations to make before renting.

Keep Renting Until You Get Settled

Young people are often discouraged from renting because it's a waste of money and they are urged to build up home equity instead. Real estate companies are persuading this age group to walk away from paying hefty rents to buying or building their own homes.

But come to think about it, buying a home only makes sense if you have stability in your life. That means if you are married, comfortable with your job prospects and have no future plans of moving anytime in the next decade.

However, most young people require flexibility when they are growing their career. In most cases, the career l may require them to move across towns and countries, when they are still in their 20's and 30's.

Therefore, buying a home at this young age means being held captive in a job or town because you have a home. Selling the home can be an option, but it will take a lot of time, money and significant transaction costs on your side as a seller.

I am not advocating that you never buy or build a home. The point I am making is that, you should never take that path, if you want flexibility in your life. Just wait until it perfectly fits into your lifestyle.

Rent should be a maximum of 30% of gross salary

When you are looking for the perfect place to rent, there are a few considerations that you should make. These may include;

✓ Distance to work
✓ Cost of the rent
✓ Old versus new
✓ Apartment versus house
✓ Size of the rental place
✓ Which utilities are included
✓ City versus town suburbs versus country side

Above all these considerations, cost should always be the overriding parameter. If it were possible to have the entire the list without thinking affordability, then everyone would gladly take that option.

So how do you figure out what you can afford?

Your rental budget should be between 25- 30% of your gross salary. This way, the balance will be enough to cater for the rest of your expenses. Extending your rental budget beyond 30% will make you make other trade-offs in your lifestyle. Yes! Because you just cannot have it all.

Let's look at it perceptively. If your gross salary is $48,000 a year, the rent should be $12,000-$14,400 a year. This translates to $1000-$1200 a month. If utility bills are added in the rent, then it can be quite affordable.

If you manage to get an ideal house that costs less than $1,000 a month, ensure that you put the extra amount in a savings account, for a future down payment towards buying a house.

Do not buy if you are not ready for responsibility

Owning a home is not for the meek. It requires a lot of time, money and energy. Buying a home through a mortgage involves a lot of paper work and tax process. All this is easy if you are renting, since the entire burden is left to the landlord. However, when you are a homeowner, you will need to handle everything by yourself. From hiring professionals, scheduling time to meet them, meet their expenses and seek reimbursements from the insurance company. If you are not ready for this headache, then you better keep renting.

Understand your right of the security deposit

It is unfortunate that most landlords view the security deposit as part of rent. I have a few friends who have lost their security deposit because the landlord failed to refund it. This happened even after taking great care of the apartment.

If the landlord fails to return the deposit, then you will have no choice but to sue him/her to get your money back. However, the entire legal process might be tedious and expensive in terms of money and time.

The best option to ensure that your security deposit remains safe, is to not pay your last month's rent. When you fail to pay the rent, the landlord will use the security deposit as the monthly rent. Thereafter, he/she can assess any damages done to the apartment and charge you for the same separately.

By using the security deposit as your last month's rent, you are simply protecting yourself against losing your hard-earned money.

THE BUYING LESSON

When you are shopping for a house, it's easy to allow the emotions control the show. Before you know it, you land in a house you cannot afford. That is a gross mistake that can affect your financial goals and your ability to build long term wealth.

Buying a house is a big investment and that explains why you cannot afford to take chances. You must get it right. Here are a few tips that will help you get it right when purchasing such as a big investment.

Buy a cheaper home than you can afford

Most real estate experts will tell you to buy an expensive home because your income will always grow. But this is a risky proportion that puts too much stress and pressure on you.

The best option would be to start by buying a cheaper house than you can afford. When your income grows, you can then embark on purchasing a nicer and a spacious home in a better neighborhood.

The good thing is that, when you buy the first home, you can save the extra income for your next home. If you invest smartly, you will soon be buying homes for cash or with a small down payment.

This strategy will ultimately help you to enjoy your young and adult years without the pressure of high mortgage and the strict responsibility that comes with owning a home.

Consider cost and location

Cost and location are the two primary determinants that should guide you towards owning a home. When it comes to location, here are the factors that need to guide you;

- ✓ **The neighborhood safety and security**- talk to the local people and get to know about crime and accident reports
- ✓ **Proximity to work** – whether you will be driving to work or using public transport, your home needs to be close to the highway and your workplace. You will be surprised how drive time can easily increase during peak hours, resulting in being late for work
- ✓ **Proximity to shopping** – I want to believe that you do not want to buy a home in a place that will require you to drive for fifteen minutes to get to the grocery store
- ✓ **Proximity to schools** – needless to say, your home should be in a place where your kids or future kids can easily get the bus service to school. If your home is located near top rated schools, it comes as a double advantage. First, for your children, quality education if they will be attending one of the schools and second for your home's resale value, if you intend to sell it off in the future.
- ✓ **Traffic** – survey the area and ensue that there is not too much traffic when going through your neighborhood.

Assuming that you can find a perfect house in one of the best and ideal locations, you will need to consider the cost of buying that home. Here are a few things to consider when it comes to pricing.

- ✓ **Do not overpay** - research widely to find out the current housing prices in the area. A good place to find such information is realtor.com.
- ✓ **Resale value** – the appreciation potential of a property is based on several factors, among them its location, as discussed above.

✓ **Utilize effective negotiation** - to ensure that you get the most competitive price, let the sellers know that you are looking at several houses in the neighborhood. It's also a good strategy to offer a price that is 10% lower than the listed price. This will create a good platform for negotiation as you can always increase your price with a small margin.

Considering that a home is one of the most important purchases you will ever make in your life, ensure that the time, effort and money you invest in it is all worth it.

EVALUATE THE HOUSE BEFORE BUYING

When buying a house, it's a no-brainer that there are specific elements that you want your home to have. Sometimes you will need to forego certain elements in the expense of others. When that happens, evaluate your second or third alternative before making the big purchase.

Below is a house evaluator guide to help you identify the house you want. Against every element you should indicate a score of 1-5 based on whether the house makes you happy or not.

General	**Score**
Location	_____
Price	_____
Year built	_____
Utility costs	_____
Extras to consider	_____

Inside	
Master bedroom	_____
Kids' rooms	_____
Play room	_____
Living room	_____
Dining room	_____
Kitchen	_____
Basement	_____

Outside	_____
Landscaping	_____
The outside appearance	_____

Kitchen area   _____
Pool area   _____
Neighborhood   _____
Noise   _____

NOTE
The scoring system
1= Deal Breaker
2= Unacceptable
3= Acceptable
4= Good
5= Great
Keep in mind that the kind of house you are looking for may not have all the elements you want. Therefore, just eliminate those from the evaluator and add the elements you want to include.

THE MORTGAGE LESSON

A mortgage is a loan that you take to buy property or land. The loan is usually secured against the value of the property, until you have fully paid the loan off. In the case where you cannot keep up your repayments, the lender has the rights to take back your property/home and sell it off to get back their money. Most often, a mortgage has a repayment period of 25 years, but this term can be adjusted to be shorter or longer.

Essentially, a mortgage has three parts; a down payment, monthly payments and fees. The monthly payment is the amount you will need to pay every month towards your mortgage. This payment includes a part of the loan principle, interest charged, property taxes and other fees.

The down payment is the upfront amount paid to secure a mortgage. If you pay a large down payment, you will get a lower interest rate, pay less fees and gain equity in your home more rapidly.

The fees usually consist of the various costs (besides the down payment) you will have to pay upfront to get your loan.

Here are a few tips to help you get the best deal for your mortgage.

Ensure that your down payment is at least 20%

Some lenders will give you a loan even when you put less than 20% as down payment. However, they will end up charging you more and this will force you to get a private mortgage insurance. The insurance is normally not a small amount and this will add more pressure to your financial goal.

Putting a 20% down payment will help you understand whether you really can afford that house. Some people pay a down payment of as little as 3% but they later find themselves in deep trouble when they cannot afford the monthly payments. It is only later that it dawns on them that the house was actually worth less than the purchase price.

Always remember that, the larger the down payment, the lower your monthly payment will be. When your monthly payments are less, it becomes easier to pay off your house - which is your main goal.

All this sums up to our earlier argument. Do not buy a house until you can afford it. This is because a mortgage is a long-term commitment that can strain you financially, if you are not well prepared.

Your Monthly payment should not exceed 28% of your gross salary

Always keep your monthly payment within your budget limit. To be on the safe side, you can bring down the 28% to any value between 20% and 25%.

Most people forget to factor in property tax, insurance and other fees in their monthly payment. This eventually leads them to paying monthly payments of more than 30%.

To bring this into perspective, let's look at this example.

- ✓ $250,000 home purchase
- ✓ $50,000 down payment (20 percent down)
- ✓ $200,000 fifteen-year mortgage (with a 6 percent interest rate)
- ✓ $1,687/month mortgage payment
- ✓ $300/month property tax ($3,600/year)
- ✓ $100/month insurance ($1,200/year)

Using this example, your monthly mortgage payment should be $2,087 (($1,687 + $300+ $100). Using the 28% rule, you will need to make an income of at least $7,500 per month to feel comfortable purchasing this home.

Many people take out mortgage loans without doing these simple calculations. Always make sure that you stay below 28% to avoid the trap of buying a more expensive house than you can afford.

Shop around for interest rates

The two main parameters that can adversely affect your mortgage payment are the interest rates and mortgage repayment length. Always shop around for the lowest rate possible without additional fees.

If this looks like a tedious activity for you, use a well-known mortgage broker to help you compare the rates and terms of different lenders. Brokers build their reputation by bringing favorable deals to borrowers. Therefore, you can be sure of a reputable broker doing a good job.

It is however important to do your research on the internet and visiting local banks to understand the terms of various institutions.

Always remember to compare your broker's rates, with what you find out and then settle for the lowest rate and best terms.

If possible, opt for a short mortgage repayment length

A shorter mortgage repayment length has two great advantages. First it assures you that you are not buying what you cannot afford. Secondly, it saves you tens of thousands of dollars.

Let's compare two mortgage plans to help you understand this better.

Option A: A fifteen-year mortgage plan
- ✓ $200,000 mortgage, fifteen-year term, 6 percent interest rate
- ✓ Monthly payment: $1,687
- ✓ Interest paid over the life of the loan: $103,788

Option B: A thirty-year mortgage
- ✓ $200,000 mortgage, thirty-year term, 6.5 percent interest rate (interest rates for thirty-year mortgages are typically at least 0.5 percent higher than those for fifteen-year mortgages)
- ✓ Monthly payment: $1,264
- ✓ Interest paid over the life of the loan: $255,089

From the above example, a fifteen-year mortgage plan saves you $423 per month compared to a thirty-year mortgage plan. Again, the fifteen-year mortgage allows you to own your home earlier yet at a lower cost. Therefore, a shorter mortgage allows you manage your budget effectively without getting into thoughts of selling your house sooner than expected.

CHAPTER 8

Take Away Notes

By now, it's my belief that you have a strong grasp of how to manage your money. Remember that personal finance is a work in progress that gets better with time. Just continue prioritizing on your financial goals and you will soon be happy with your financial life.

Here are a few important tips that summarize our entire discussion in this book

Budgeting
- ✓ Invest in a filing system to keep track of all your financial records.
- ✓ Whenever you get a pay rise or unexpected income, ensure that you save a big part of it.
- ✓ Build an emergency fund that covers at least six months of your purchases.

Saving
- ✓ Always bring your lunch to work as often as possible.
- ✓ Learn how to fix household things by yourself instead of calling a handy man all the time.

Spending
- ✓ Don't try to keep up with the Joneses. They are going bankrupt.
- ✓ Drop unhealthy spending habits.
- ✓ Generic drugs and medications are as good as the brand names.
- ✓ Do not purchase the first generation of a product. Wait for the second, third and fourth, since the cost will have dropped.
- ✓ Buy quality surge protectors for your expensive electronics.
- ✓ Extended warranties on cars, televisions, electronics and appliances are not worth it. Do not buy them.

Investing
- ✓ Beware of investing your time and money in multi-level marketing programs and get-rich quick schemes.
- ✓ Never make oral agreements with friends and family members for any significant purchases and sales.

✓ Diversify your investment portfolio to distribute your risk and gains uniformly.

Debts

✓ Instead of taking a car loan, wait until you can afford to buy a new one.

✓ Use credit cards smartly to avoid getting into bad debt.

✓ If possible, always use cash instead of credit cards. It will help you feel the impact of your spending.

Insurance

✓ Always read your insurance manual cover to cover.

✓ Always opt for the highest deductible for your home and automobile insurance.

✓ It is important to identify the essential insurance covers that you need and those that you do not.

Housing

✓ If it is offered, trade off the big wedding with a house down payment.

✓ Unless you are settled, do not buy. If you cannot afford it, do not buy. Continue renting.

✓ If possible, pay a high down payment for your mortgage and opt for a plan with a short repayment period.

✓ Your rent should never exceed 30% of your gross salary.

THANK YOU NOTE

I want to thank you for purchasing and reading this book. It is my hope that you have learnt a lot from it.

However, you must recognize that you are the only person responsible for your own financial success or failure. If you heed the advice in this book and develop your own principles, then   it is very possible for you to effectively manage your financial life.

Can I ask you for a quick favor?

If you enjoyed reading this book, please leave a positive review on Amazon. I love getting feedback from my readers and reviews on Amazon will make a great difference.

I read all the reviews and therefore would appreciate to hear your thoughts.

Thank you so much!

May Collins

ABOUT THE AUTHOR

The author, May Collins is a seasoned writer and a money and wealth coach. She uses her expertise to educate the middle-class Americans better and shows proper ways to handle money, by making smart investments and staying out of debt.

Printed in Great Britain
by Amazon